POETS NOW

Edited by Robert Peters

GET HOT OR GET OUT

A Selection of Poems, 1957-1981

by Jonathan Williams

adi et omo!
—Cutallus

Poets Now **1**

The Scarecrow Press, Inc.
Metuchen, N.J., & London   1982

Jonathan Williams has made this selection of his poems from six fugitive, high-risk volumes that have come and gone:

AN EAR IN BARTRAM'S TREE (University of North Carolina Press, 1969; reissued in paperback by New Directions, 1972).

BLUES & ROOTS/RUE & BLUETS (Grossman, 1971).

THE LOCO LOGODAEDALIST IN SITU (Cape Goliard/Grossman, 1972).

ELITE/ELATE POEMS (The Jargon Society, Highlands, 1979).

GLEES . . . SWARTHY MONOTONIES . . . RINCE COCHON . . . & CHOZZERAI FOR SIMON . . . (DBA Editions, Roswell, 1980, privately published).

HOMAGE UMBRAGE QUIBBLE & CHICANE (DBA Editions, Roswell, 1981, privately published).

JW would like to thank the following publishers and editors who sponsored or worked on the above books: Lambert Davis, Leslie Phillabaum, James Laughlin, Richard Grossman, Michael Loeb, Barry Hall, Tom Maschler, Donald B. Anderson, and Joseph Anderson.

JW also thanks Edmund White, in his *States of Desire*, for GET HOT OR GET OUT. It seems that this cathectic sign hangs over the dance floor of "The Brazos River Bottom," a bar for that endangered species, the gay cowboy, in Houston, Texas.

Library of Congress Cataloging in Publication Data

Williams, Jonathan.
  Get hot or get out.

  (Poets now   ; no. 1)
  I. Title. II. Series.
PS3545.I52966A6   1982   811'.54   81-18398
ISBN 0-8108-1495-1   AACR2

INTRODUCTION

If prophets are blessed with having a third eye, some poets are gifted with a third ear, affixed symbolically to the back of the skull, to catch spleen and sounds not sufficiently registered at the sides. If this Magritte-like image makes sense, it does particularly for Jonathan Williams, whose perceptions of the speech of others is amazingly keen. Williams is antiquarian, and, at the same time, very modern ("postquarian"). His poems are often taken from gravestones (Part 1 is called "Celebrations on Stones"), or from billboards and signs—the materials of popular culture. At other times, he is the antiquarian sleuth, recording scraps of North Carolina and English folk-speech; he is a Johnny Appleseed of poetry who hears, records, and fertilizes our imaginations and feelings. In painting, one thinks of Stuart Davis's work, but of a Davis derived from the rural and bucolic rather than the urban.

Williams is a poet of the democratic urge who respects folk sources. He seems to imply that without returns to these roots there can be no vital literary language. Nevertheless, he is a poet of fairly esoteric tastes—in composers, writers, and artists; and his word-magic reflects the ebullient psyche of a sophisticated man who also cares about elitist culture, and about language used in its most demanding forms. These extremes account for much of his originality; for his exuberance, wit, intelligence, and empathy are unique in contemporary poetry. Reading him well requires alertness; he's apt to put something delicious over on you when you aren't looking. He is also a voice for social tolerance. While he has fun with the English public-school tradition of boy-love, the portion of this book he calls "The Sexual Strut," invites and nourishes the open mind toward deviations from sexual norms. His attacks on the Rev. McIntire, Anita Bryant, George Wallace, and Lester Maddox are scathingly funny.

In a sense, his long poem inspired by Charles Ives (Part 4)—the most original and folk-anchored composer America has so far produced—reveals more of Williams's origins than anything else he has written. Like Ives, Williams is not enamored of the highly polished, traditional art form; just as one finds beauty in a crudely fashioned North Carolina bird house or in an English country stile, so there is beauty in the carpentered free-verse poem tacked and glued to the page. As his poems show, Williams, again like Ives, is a disciple of the great American Transcendentalists. There's some of the spunk, energy, and fearless eschewing of popular ideas one associates with Henry Thoreau and Walt Whitman, and, to a lesser degree, with Emerson.

Williams is both a minimalist and an expansive poet. He writes some of the best one-line poems around; and his "improvisations," written while listening to Ives, Bruckner, and Mahler, reflect the structures of these composers, requiring as much time to absorb as listening to their music does.

I am certain that *Get Hot or Get Out* will find the readers it deserves. He has been too long inaccessible—out of print, or available only in private edi-

iv

tions. He is in the mainstream of American writing, and we are pleased to feature him first in our series.

Finally, his seminal contributions to American letters, in his appropriately named Jargon Press, are unparalleled. For thirty years, he has been publishing books by other poets, first-voices who are now major American writers—Charles Olson, Robert Creeley, Denise Levertov, Robert Duncan, Michael McClure. He resurrected Louis Zukofsky, Lorine Niedecker, Alfred Starr Hamilton, Walter Lowenfels, and Mina Loy after generations of neglect. He was also one of the first small-press publishers to wander the country selling his exquisite volumes literally from door to door and from store to store. I am happy to report that there is no sign of a let-up in his energies.

Robert Peters
Editor, *Poets Now*

CONTENTS

1. Celebrations on Stones

2. The Southern Mountains

5. The Sexual Strut

6. A Democracy of Content; or, "Some People Would Write About Anything"

CELEBRATIONS ON STONES

GAIUS VALERIUS CATULLUS

I love and I hate
and that's all she wrote!

JACK SPICER

there was his poem
about the ugly gardener's son,
Crotchety Priapus,

weary in the weeds without the hots
for anyone

let's hope Death
has a big one
for Jack

SIR EDWARD ELGAR

went wyde in this world wondres to here —
hill tune and wind song with Maluerne's* ear

----

*this spelling of Wm Langland's medieval demesne is according
 to the Rev. Skeats*

CHARLES IVES

Where O
Where
are
the Pea-Green
Freshmen?

New Haven,
West Redding, and
Heaven!

All aboard!

Amen!

LEOŠ JANÁČEK

I wanted to sink my eye
into the blue of the sky

BUNK JOHNSON

he died
like the moon

fading out white
before day

CARL NIELSEN

as if all the world
sang one fine tune!

CHARLIE PARKER

turn on the Bird, the Bird
turns me on, even
the Early Bird
turns worms

FRANCIS POULENC

ô salades!
ô mes délices!

ô Sally!
ô Alice!

salut!
ô zut
alors!

ERIK SATIE

sat at tea

JEAN SIBELIUS

the drone of overtones in
a rye field by
a river

SOLOMON'S LAMENT FOR STEFAN WOLPE

For, lo, the winter is past,
the rain is over
and gone. . .

o Jerusalem,
saw ye him whom my soul loveth?

the force
to set
anemones
on fire

tell him,
I am sick of love

ELEGY FOR A PHOTOGRAPH
OF WILLIAM CARLOS WILLIAMS

the last, absolutely the Last
Dahlia

on Ridge Road, Rutherford, New Jersey, October 18,
 1960—

you have outlived It,
and wear the Epaulet
to prove it. . .

I salute you in your
Garden State!

You taught us to
scrape all the Leaves off the Bottom of the Barrel,
because the Leaves can equal

the Sacred Red Anemones of Osiris
falling in the Blue Waterfalls of
Lebanon—

and you knew it

A VALEDICTION FOR MY FATHER
(1898–1974)

all the old things
are gone now

and the people are
different

IMITATION COCKNEY HOMAGE TO FLAUBERT

just a mot
juste

PHILIP HOPE-WALLACE (1911–1979)

Gentlemen I must
report from a visit
to Lesbos

the natives are Lesbians
to a man

SPRING THAW
AT THE OLD GOODMAN PLACE
(for Paul)

    THE MORE
    YOU COME

    THE MORE
    YOU CAN!

MUSE-FLASH
FOR RALPH EUGENE MEATYARD

    come on,
    Gene

    the
    Boogers
    got

    Lummy Jean Licklighter

    in an attic
    over near Viper!

UNITARIAN CRI DE GUERRE, CHEZ POINT, VIENNE (ISÈRE)

du Beurre!
donnez-moi du Beurre!
toujours de Beurre!

STILL WATER
FOR LORINE NIEDECKER (1903–1970)

she seined words
as others stars
or carp

laconic as
a pebble
in the Rock River

along the bank
where the peony flowers
fall

her tall friend
the pine tree
is still there

to see

AN OMEN FOR STEVIE SMITH
"Being alive is like being in enemy territory."

this is your Aunt, Stevie,
and oh you must hurry!

The Man in Black
who waits tonight along the Lyke Wake Walk
has a gown for you
the colour of rowan berries;

a gown borne in air by hornets,
hagworms and ants, riding
the backs of great bustards and herons. . .

your cats,
Brown and Fry and Hyde,
yes, Stevie, they too
shall come at last
to Whinny-Moor. . .

the five of you
shall dance that heath
to Death

FROM UNCLE JAKE CARPENTER'S
ANTHOLOGY OF DEATH
ON THREE-MILE CREEK

Loney Ollis
age 84
dide jun 10 1871

grates dere honter
wreked bee trees for hony
cild ratell snak by 100
cild dere by thousen

i nod him well

THE EPITAPH
ON UNCLE NICK GRINDSTAFF'S GRAVE
ON THE IRON MOUNTAIN
ABOVE SHADY VALLEY, TENNESSEE:

LIVED ALONE   SUFFERED ALONE   DIED ALONE

PAINT SIGN ON A ROUGH ROCK
YONSIDE OF BOONE SIDE
OF SHADY VALLEY

BEPREPA

REDTO

MEETGO

D

FARMER BERESFORD, ON NOBILITY IN LANGSTROTHDALE CHASE

if thou piss free,
fart dry,
and pay 20 shillings in t' pound,

no man can touch thee!

SHEPHERD

I could tell he were gone,
his eye were cold

just like when you tell a dead lamb's,
it were like that

A.L.B. (1917–1978)

he was
oald as the fells
street as an arske's arse
sharp as whins
whick as a lop
wild as winter thunner
nice as an otter

and his throat war middlen slippy
and he is deed as a steann

but not gone
but not gone

Old Cumbrian Dialect —
fells: hills
street: straight
arske: an aquatic salamander or lizard, confused with *asp*
whins: gorse
whick: lively
lop: a bed flea
middlen: a fair amount

THE SOUTHERN MOUNTAINS

BEA HENSLEY HAMMERS
AN IRON CHINQUAPIN LEAF
ON HIS ANVIL NEAR SPRUCE PINE
& COGITATES ON THE NATURE OF
TWO BEAUTY SPOTS

in the Linville Gorge I
know this place

now it's a rock wall
you look up
it's covered in punktatum all
the way to Heaven

that's a
sight

●

up on Smoky
you ease up at daybust
and see the first
light in the tops of the tulip trees

now boys that just naturally
grinds and polishes
the soul

makes it
normal
again

I mean it's really
pretty!

DADDY BOSTAIN, THE MOSES OF THE WING COMMUNITY MOONSHINERS, LAMENTS FROM HIS DEATHBED THE SPIRITUAL ESTATE OF ONE OF HIS SOUL-SAVING NEIGHBORS:

God bless her pore
little ol
dried up
soul!

jest make
good kindlin wood
fer Hell. . .

OLD MAN SAM WARD'S HISTORY
OF THE GEE'HAW WHIMMY-DIDDLE

some folks say
the injuns made 'em
like lie-detectors
called 'em
hoo-doo sticks

feller
in Salisbury, Noth Caylini
made the first
whimmy-diddle I seen

I whittle seven
kind: thisuns king
size, thisuns jumbo, thisuns
extry large

here's a single, here's one
double, here's a triple and why right here
here's a forked 'un

been whittlin' whimmy-diddles come
ten year, I reckon you'd
care to see my other toys,
boys, I got some fine
flippers-dingers, fly-
killers and bull-roarers, I can

kill a big fly at 60 feet

watch here

THE HERMIT CACKLEBERRY BROWN, ON HUMAN VANITY:

caint call your name
but your face is easy

come sit

now some folks figure theyre
bettern
cowflop they
aint

not a bit

just good to hold the world together
like hooved up ground

thats what

LEE OGLE TIES A BROOM & PONDERS CURES FOR ARTHURITIS

lands them fingers really
dreadfulled me I
couldnt tie
nary broom one

had to soak em in water
hot as birds blood

then I heard this ol man from Kentucky say
take a jug of apple juice just juice not cider
pour the epsum salts to it and
take as much as you kin

bein fleshy I kin take
right smart but
boys you know it moves a mans bowels
somethin terrible

well boys it just
naturally killed that arthuritis
lost me some weight too
and I
still tie thesehere brooms

pretty good

SNUFFY SMITH'S COLOSSAL MAW
FROM WAR-WOMAN DELL

more mouth on
that woman

than ass
on a goose

THE CUSTODIAN OF A FIELD OF WHISKEY BUSHES BY THE NOLICHUCKY RIVER SPEAKS:

took me a pecka real ripe tomaters up
into the Grassy Gap
one night

and two quarts of good stockade
and just laid there

sippin and tastin and lookin agin the moon
at them sorta fish eyes in the jar
you get when its right

boys Im talkin bout somethin
good

A RIDE IN A BLUE CHEVY
FROM ALUM CAVE TRAIL
TO NEWFOUND GAP

goin' hikin'?
git in!

o the Smokies are ok but me
I go for Theosophy,
higher things, Hindu-type philosophy,
none of this licker and sex, I
like it
on what we call the astral plane,
I reckon I get more i-thridral
by the hour

buddy, you won't believe this but
how old you reckon the earth is?
the earth is
precisely 156 trillion years old —
I got this book from headquarters in
Wheaton, Illinois
says it is!

I'll tell you somethin' else:
there are exactly 144 kinds of people on this earth—
12 signs and the signs change
every two hours,
that's 144, I'm Scorpio,
with Mars over the water

here's somethin' else innerestin':
back 18 million years
people was only one sex, one sex only. . .
I'd like to explain that,
it's right here in this pamphlet,
50 cents. . .

never married, lived with my mother in Ohio,
she died, I'm over in Oak Ridge
in a machine shop, say,
what kind of place
is Denver?
think I'll sell this car, go to Denver,
set up a Center. . .

name's Davis,
what's yours?

AUNT CREASY, ON WORK:

shucks
I make the livin

uncle
just makes the livin
worthwhile

THE ANCIENT OF DAYS

would that I
had known Aunt Cumi
Woody

C-u-m-i, pronounced
Q-my

she lived in the Deyton Bend Section of Mitchell
County, North Carolina many years ago

there is one of Bayard Wootten's photographs of her
standing there with her store-bought
teeth, holding a coverlet

she sheared her sheep, spun
and dyed her yarn in vegetable dyes,
and wove the coverlet

in indigo, the brown from walnut roots,
red from madder, green from hickory ooze, first,
then into the indigo (the blue pot)

Cumi, from the Bible
(St. Mark 5:41)

Talitha Cumi:
"Damsel, I say unto thee, arise!"

she is gone, she
enjoyed her days

THE SEPTEMBER SATISFACTION
OF UNCLE IV OWENS:

    I got
    a rat-proof
    crib!

UNCLE IV SURVEYS HIS DOMAIN FROM
HIS ROCKER OF A SUNDAY AFTERNOON
AS AUNT DORY STARTS TO CHOP
THE KINDLIN

    Mister Williams
    lets youn me move
    tother side the house

    the woman
    choppin woods
    mite nigh the awkerdist thing
    I seen

THREE SAYINGS FROM HIGHLANDS,
NORTH CAROLINA:

but pretty though as
roses is
you can put up with
the thorns

Doris Talley, Housewife & Gardener

you live until you die —
if the limb don't fall

Butler Jenkins, Caretaker

your points is blue
and your timing's
a week off

Sam Creswell, Auto Mechanic

CRACKER-BARREL REVERIES
ON THE TUNE "PAX AMERICANA"
"Us common people run this country!"
—George Wallace

feller over in
franklin
says hes got thishere book
says that fbi feller hoover
says that nigger preacher kings
nothin
but a tarnation communist

and i reckon you boys
heared on the tv this
walter jenkins hes
some kind of unnatchrul sex prevert why
you know them seven chillun
must be lightbulbs
you just know it

just like you know ol castro
and them jew boys in new york
got us into veetnam

some things bes plain obvious

why the barber feller was sayin
just yesterday
he said put the bombs to em boys drop em
all over them russkis and
the dadblame chinamens too and
might as well drop em on old dee gawl
too hes got the big mouth dont he

i mean put it to em all
i mean buddy we could stop all this foolishness up north

why some things bes plain obvious

people get
what they want

COBWEBBERY

*"The spirit and the will survived, but something
in the soul perished."* —D.H. Lawrence

the best spiders for soup
are the ones under
stones —

ask the man who is one:
plain white american

(not blue gentian red indian yellow sun black caribbean)

hard heart, cold
mind's found

a home
in the ground

"a rolling stone, *nolens volens*,
ladles no soup"

maw, rip them boards off
the side the house

and put the soup pot on

and plant us some petunias
in the carcass of the Chevrolet

and let's stay here
and rot in the fields

and sit still

The Lawrence quote is from his introduction to Edward Dahlberg's first novel, Bottom Dogs *(City Lights, 1961). He spoke of the American character . . . "nolens volens": willy-nilly.*

DEALER'S CHOICE
AND THE DEALER SHUFFLES
(for William Burroughs)

I saw the Chattahoochee River get a haircut.
I saw Fidel Castro flow softly towards Apalachicola,
    Florida.

I saw a bank of red clay integrate with Jesuits.
I saw Bob Jones Bible University used to make baked
    flamingos.

I saw the Governor of Mississippi join the NAACP.
I saw a black gum tree refuse to leaf and go to jail.

I saw the DAR singing *"We Shall Overcome!"*
I saw Werner von Braun knitting gray (and brown) socks
    for the National Guard.

I saw the Motto of Alabama: "IT'S TOO WET TO
    PLOUGH!"
I saw God tell Adam: "WE DARE DEFEND OUR
    RIGHTS!"

I saw the City of Albany fried in deep fat.
I saw eight catfish star on Gomorrah TV.

I saw "THE INVASION OF THE BODY-SNATCHERS"
    at the Tyger Drive-In.
I saw William Blake grow like a virus in the sun.

I saw the South suckin hind titty.
I saw the North suckin hind titty.

I saw a man who saw these too
And said though strange they were all true.

Postface:

"There was a crow sat on a clod—
And now I've finished my sermon, thank God."

HEART-SONG
DEAR TO THE AMERICAN PEOPLE

don't let the sun set on your head! I said
to the golden rod

it stood
in the pine wood

out back
it was black

as a heart

DEAR REVEREND CARL C. McINTIRE:

Just a note
to let you know
we are listening to you
on Station
K-I-K-E
in Richmond,
Virginia

There are four of us Fundamentalist Baptist ladies
who ride to work together at 7:30
to the shirt factory and the napalm plant
and we always listen to your
"20TH CENTURY REFORMATION HOUR"
every day
after the early morning
"MO-TOWN-SOUND-SHOW" with
"Urethra & the Catheters" —

you both groove, baby,
I mean you let it *all* hang out
and no doubt!

So when you laid that wicked-world bit
on our heads Friday we felt we should be prepared
to meet God and goodness we sure would feel lost
without your spiritual uplift in our new pink
Dodge Polara. . .

Yours agin sin and keep keeping those darkies
from destroying our freedom,
zang-a-dang!

Myrtle Jean Pugh, Co-Captain
James River Industrial League of
White Women Bowlers,
Team # 16

STANDING BY HIS TRAILER-STUDIO
IN CAMPTON, KENTUCKY,
EDGAR TOLSON WHITTLES
A FEW SYLLABLES
(for Ellsworth Taylor)

that piece
thats what some folks call a *spinach*
or some damn thing

i got it
offn a match box

it needs wings
and a lions tail

some damn woman down in Lexington
wants it

WHO IS LITTLE ENIS?

Little Enis is
"one hunnert an' 80lbs of
dynamite
with a 9-inch
fuse."

his real name is
Carlos Toadvine
which his wife Irma Jean
pronounces *Carlus*

Carlos says
Toadaveenie is a eyetalyun name,
used to be lots of 'em
round these parts

Ed McClanahan is the World's Leading Little Enis Freak
and all this information comes to you from a weekend
        in Winston
with Big Ed telling the lore of Lexington, Kentucky,
which is where Enis has been hanging it out for years
        and years,
at *Boots Bar* and *Giuseppe's Villa* and, now,
        The Embers,
pickin' and singin' rockabilly style.

Carlus ain't what he was
according to Irma Jean's accounts
(and even to his own):

he was sittin' there one night in the kitchen at home
tellin' stories and talkin' trash about Irma Jean —
with her right there with her hair put up in them pink
        plastic curlers —
about how these days he likes to pop it to her dog-style
just now and again and how she likes it pretty damn well
when they wander all over the house
and end up in the living room corner —
"I'm just afraid Carlus will run us out the door and
        down the street
opposite the automatic laundry. . ."

The 9-inch fuse hung down Enis' left leg
is called, familiarly,
Ol'Blue

Ol'Blue used to be in the pink! —
way in. . .

Blue has a head on him like a tom-cat
and ribs like a hongry hound

and he used to get so hard
a cat
couldn't
scratch it. . .

But now that Enis has the cirrhosis
and take all thesehere harmones
Ol'Blue just don't
stand up
like a little man
and cut the mustard
anymore

But Enis will smile and say
let's all have a drink, maybe I can drown thatthere liver
    of ours,
it's no bigger'n a dime nohow anymore, it just floats
    in there. . .

Hey, Blue, let's shake that thang!
Turn a-loose this oldie
by my boy Elvis—
a golden oldie!
let's go, Blue!

And off they go
into the Wild Blue
Yonder in the Blue
Grass. . .

Carlos & Blue,
thinking of you. . .

Hail & Farewell

NIGHT LANDSCAPE IN NELSON COUNTY, KENTUCKY

ah, Moon, shine
thou as amber in thy
charred-keg, hickory sky . . .

still as a still, steep
as a horse's face

LECONTE HIGH-TOP

under the rondelay
the sun

into the wind and rain a
winter wren

again, again—

its song
needling the pines

DAVENPORT GAP

the tulip poplar is not a
poplar it is a magnolia:
liriodendron tulipifera

the young grove on the eastern slopes of
Mt. Cammerer reminds me
of the two huge trees
at Monticello, favorites
of Mr. Jefferson;

and of the Virginia lady
quoting Mr. Kennedy:

the recent gathering of
Nobel Prize Winners at the
White House — the most
brilliant assemblage
in the dining room
since Mr. Jefferson
dined there

alone. . .

a liriodendron
wind, a liriodendron
mind

THE FLOWER-HUNTER IN THE FIELDS

a flame azalea, mayapple, maple, thornapple
plantation

a white cloud in the eye
of a white horse

a field of bluets moving
below the black suit
of William Bartram

bluets, or "Quaker Ladies," or some say
"Innocence"

bluets and the blue of gentians and
Philadelphia blue laws!

high hills,

stone cold
sober

as October

THE DERACINATION

definition: *root*,

"a growing point,
an organ of absorption, an aereating organ,
a good reservoir, or
means of support"

Vernonia glauca, order *Compositae*,
"these tall perennials with
corymbose cymes of bright-purple heads of
tubular flowers
with conspicuous stigmas"

I do not know the Ironweed's root,
but I know it rules September

and where the flowers tower
in the wind there is a burr of
sound—empyrean . . . the mind
glows and the wind drifts. . .

epiphanies pull up
from roots —

epiphytic, making it up

out of the air

PLINTH

bronze

of galax
leaf

in Leach's
celadon

on
bronze

AN AUBADE FROM VERLAINE'S DAY
(for Alfred Stieglitz)

the cloud in my head
wide to the edge of the world

the level cloud
that fills the Valley of the Little Tennessee
from Ridgepole to Rabun Bald

the laughter of
the Lord God Bird
Who pecks
berries
from the
dogwood

makes these two clouds
one, one eye
open

JEFF BROOKS,
WAGON-MASTER OF ANDREWS,
EN ROUTE TO FRANKLIN
THROUGH THE NANTAHALAS:

no
other
sound

except

the creak
of leather

HOMAGE
TO THE REVEREND A. RUFUS MORGAN,
ON MOUNT LECONTE AT 92

Rufus

you reckon there's
anything in Heaven

worth climbing
173 times?

A BLUE RIDGE WEATHER PROPHET
MAKES TWELVE STITCHES IN TIME
ON THE TWELFTH DAY OF CHRISTMAS

January

worst
winter

since
last!

.

February

if the catbirds chatter
winter's mite nigh over

and spring is just around the corner but
we aint seen the corner yet

.

March

sap-risin'
time
is lovin'
time,

o supine pine

.

April

this aint
blackberry winter

this is
late Easter squirt

.

May

good time
to plant corn

when the hickory buds
are as big
as a squirrel's foot

.

June

when you tend
to your
own business
you got
a load,

come rain or come
shine

.

July

heavy
elder
bloom—

good
old time
sign

.

August

hit's frost
6 weeks from
when
the katydids
holler

.

September

elder people said that gnat swarms
were a good sign of thunder storms

but since then,
only some light rain. . .

.

October

heavy black
on the front end
of the woolly worm

bad weather
in the first go-round
of winter time

.

November

first snow

get out,
wade in it
a little bit

old people, now dead,
said

.

December

if you would rather see mild weather
and see some sign that makes you sorter
think a little bit it
is going to be a mild winter
it will make you at least for a little while feel
better about it—

before the real begins!

AUBADE

you could hear an ant
fart
it was that
quiet

IVES

A CELESTIAL CENTENNIAL REVERIE
FOR CHARLES EDWARD IVES
The Man Who Found Our Music In The Ground
(for Herbert Leibowitz)

In 1944 Arnold Schoenberg wrote a tribute (undelivered) that said: "There is a great Man living in this country—a composer. . ." Name: Charles E. Ives. Which sets me to thinking about other great Men. Did Mr. Stieglitz know Mr. Ives? Did either know about Louis Sullivan? Which one knew Ezra Pound? I'm pretty sure none of them knew about Henry Clews, who had already given up on the hostility of the New York idioti and taken refuge in a villa on the Bay of Cannes. The verdict on Mr. Clews, our Rodin/Medardo Rosso/H.P. Lovecraft of sculpture, is not yet in. The others occupied this giant vacant land during roughly the same decades—before drink, sickness, exile, depression set in on them.

Being in the unenviable position of hardly being able to distinguish an okra pod from C-sharp, what precisely is it that I may presume to add to the wisdom of this *omnium gatherum* of Ives People? Well, I have been collecting the records for nearly 30 years. I mean 22 Ives LPs—same number as I have of Miles Davis, if that means anything. I have just been reading all the books. Over the years I have engaged a lot of the authorities in small talk: Carl Ruggles,

Lou Harrison, John Kirkpatrick, William Masselos, Peter Yates, Wilfrid Mellers, Paul Zukofsky, Gilbert Chase, Harry Partch, Henry Brant. The poet, as ever, has little to offer but the veracity of his ears and eyes, in the hope he has kept them sharp and affectionate. If nothing else, this is one literary man who is more than willing to put up with the chaff in the grain that the latest batch of Manhattan criticasters is beginning to report on in the work of Ives.

So, I am going to give Mr. Ives a close reading, centered on the "memos" to the *Concord Sonata*. In the first instance I am going to quote the gists I like best from what I have found. Then, moving to the *Essays Before a Sonata*, I am going to work motifs I find there into new forms. Each page will be scrutinized. Some will be skip-read in the manner taught me by the photographer Frederick Sommer. Mr. Ives will be re-phrased, his words pushed around —there may be something there he didn't quite realize he was aiming at. I'll make my own noises—with some of his words. Which rather turns the tables on Cantankerous Charlie. . . . It's interesting to speculate: did C.E.I. ever write tunes of his own in his larger works?—or simply use his good shortstop's hands to peg the routine grounders in a multitude of daring directions? He threw smoke, that we know. That New England haze as unheard of, previously, as Delius's winds soughing over the Yorkshire moors. Both of them out-of-doors men; boyish; longing for the old times.

I trust that John Kirkpatrick, Howard Boatwright, Vivian Perlis, Peter Yates, Henry & Sidney Cowell, C.E.I., and diverse publishers will not be distressed by these knucklers, sleights of eye, and jug-handled curves . . . After all, I am coming in very late in the game. It is nice to recollect that Ives wrotes most of *Essays Before a Sonata* in my hometown, Asheville, North Carolina in early 1919. Forty-six years later, another lefty gets a chance in the same Blue Ridge Mountains. Maybe I'll crowd this jug-eared Yankee jock with Eli Yale just a little at the plate? Being a poet is almost as terrible as being a composer in that odd manly world Ives fretted about so. I, too, am proud of my eight varsity letters from prep-school. I keep up my hiking, volley ball, and pingpong, to keep them drug-crazed hip-pie freak students of mine in their place. Two hundred and ten pounds keep the anthropoid adults at their distance.

Part One: ZAT'S THAT ROLLO!

". . . first the eye, then the ear. And why not in music—yeah Art!—in serious music too, a something which comes up from the life of a day, perhaps something that nature does to an Elm Tree, something as of old-time humor, or a sense of hilarity, a jump-forward feeling a boy may have on an early winter morning—why not?"

"If he drawls like a Yankee and doesn't imitate an English up-inflect, but speculates ever on the Eternities, he may be as universal as Jupiter—but Arthur will just hear his drawl and put a nice label on it . . . There has to be a tag on a bushel of potatoes to be shipped . . ."

"The footnote in English words at the bottom of this page is the only thing in the Sonata that most of these dress shirts can read."

"Some nice people object to putting attempted pictures of American authors and their literature in a thing called a sonata, but I don't apologize for it or explain it. I tried it because I felt like trying, and so, Good night shirt! Rollo!"

". . . one day, when a man becomes of age, the ear begins to sit up and think for itself—and somehow that imperfect triad seems to grow less imperfect, and those two leading tones (or rather being led by tonic supremacy) get tired of that, some of that, semitone groove back home, etc.,—and the melodic tendency scolds, for the smoothness and correctness of the whole resolution is endangered. But the ear begins to look for more trails up the mountain. Thus it's now more than a resolution that's endangered—all music is endangered!—Rollo told me so."

". . . let the music move as the mountain does . . ."

"And so, when I get these letters, comments, and ree-marks of the old-made-male-ladies, it sore reminds me of what Jermimah said to Father (or Uncle Lyman, I think) after reading *Tom Sawyer*—'I don't believe half he (Mark Twain) says—he's nothin' but foolin' all the time. He ought to be more serious—he ought to learn to write good!"

"Often what is called awkward is easily called unmusical—a good hurdler doesn't have a pole to help him over—let the muscles of the hand get as strong as the Concord muscle of 1840, et al—and perhaps the muscles of the ear and soul will join in."

". . . you don't have to play everything and piece and measure the same every time—not as Josey Hofmann et al play Beethoven, this nice little note just this way, etc.—Ta ta—making Beethoven a lady-bird etc . . .

Play it before breakfast like ___________!
Play it after breakfast like___________!
Play it after digging potatoes like________!"

"For the most part, the Sonata was decided and sensed to a great extent by the ear and mind (to say nothing of the left side of the breast) before much went down on paper."

"I remember, just after finishing the 'Emerson' movement,

playing it to an old friend of mine. He said, 'That music is homely, awkward, and lanky—so was Emerson. It won't please the ladies much—neither did Emerson.' "

Part Two: ESSAYS BEFORE A SONATA

Prologue . . .

(1)   can a tune
      literally represent a stone
      wall with
      vines on it or even
      nothing
      on it?

(2)   "the nearer we get to the mere
      expression of emotion,
      says Professor Sturt in the *Philosophy*
      of Art and Personality,

      as in the antics of boys
      who have been promised a holiday,
      the further we get
      away from art"

(3)   from his definition of art
      a kick in the back
      is a work of art,
      and Beethoven's *Ninth Symphony*
      is not

      . . . those meadows
      and the woods

      so pure and bright a light
      as would have
      waked the dead . . .

(4)   the word *inspire*
      is used here:

      what will you substitute
      for the mountain lake,
      for his friend's character, etc?
      will you substitute anything?
      if so, why?
      if so, what?

      what is behind it all?
      "The Voice of God,"
      says the artist;
      "The voice of the devil,"
      says the man in the front row

(5) *"brought me there
brought you"*

(6) one hearing, or
a century of hearings . . .

a feeling
that all
is left
unsaid . . .

they seem to stand
about as they did

they use
the same words

they go on

Emerson . . .

(1) every ultimate fact
only the first of a new series
of immensities:

a seer, when seriously
left alone,

who would then discover
the wondrous chain
links the heavens
with earth

(2)   there is a chance
this guide
could not retrace his steps
if he tried
and why
should he?

(3)   modernism is an anachronism
and is as futile as
calling today's sunset modern

(4)   he hacks his way up and down:
he makes us feel that we are free to do so;
seeing the signpost to Erebus,
strong enough to go the other way

(5)   originality works
down through the crust
towards the first fire,

when a thousand
wrought like one

(6) all the religion we have
     is the ethics of one or another holy person;

     as soon as character appears,
     be sure love will,

     and veneration,
     and anecdotes and fables about him . . .

(7) the personal unit
     is the universal

     in this world,
     also in the next

     an error
     somewhere

(8) a gangplank
     (an overinterest, not
     an underinterest)

     of what
     will it
     be composed?

(9) letting
     a common experience of a day
     translate
     what is stirring
     in the soul

(10) great, dim
     outlines of Emerson

     fulfilled

(11) means

     potencies

     affinities

     signs

     new objects

     flow
     from

     devotion

(12) thoughts surge
     to his mind

     he fills heavens
     with them

     crowds them
     in, seldom arranges them

     along the ground first

     mud may be
     a form of sincerity

     daybreak
     cannot be explained

     at noon

(13) inspiration
     all gone up
     in sounds . . .

     a home run
     at evening

(14) the intellect
     is never a whole;
     it is where the soul
     finds things:

     the rivers, in thought,
     stream through us

(15) somewhere
     between jowl and soul

     beguiling

     a few sensual
     mortals

(16) uncovers a
     deformed foot,
     gives it a name

     somehow
     like to
     mix it up
     with sin

(17) space nothing!
     want all material!
     convert all impediments
     into instruments!

be hoarse as
earth-beat, sea-beat, heart-beat —

the time
to which
the sun rolls

and the globule
of blood

and the sap
of the trees

(18) instead of inspiration
the aeroplane sails o'er the
mountain

a spray of tobacco juice
falls on the poet . . .

easy for a hog,
even a stupid one,
to step on a box of matches
under a tenement with a thousand souls as
under an empty bird-house

(19) the existence of
     personal or public property
     may not prove
     the existence of God . . .

     God is on the side
     of the majority

     God has made men
     better than man . . .

     pride puts in
     its word:

     hog-mind
     is pride

(20) A Gospel hymn
     of simple devotion
     comes out to him

     through autumn
     fields
     of sumac and aster

(21) wild native Orpheus
     from what obscurity

who measures
the wonder of a moment

whence cometh
melodies

flowing now
through all our hearts

divinely
ravaging

(22) the hunger of a lifetime
     sometimes
     by one meal . . .

(23) look at flowers
     look at them alone

     look at botany alone:
     see nothing

(24) behold
     Our Leaders!

     skins thick,
     wits slick,
     hands quick!

(25) he thought
     everybody
     was as good
     as he was

     great soul
     incarnated
     in some poor ——————   . . .

     get mops!
     scrub floors!

(26) four notes
     at the beginning of
     the *Fifth Symphony*, knocking
     at the common heart
     of Concord

Hawthorne . . .

(1) his intellectual masks
     would weave his spell
     over us

     unlike something I had heard of Ravel
     whose music is of a kind
     I cannot stand:

pleasing enough,
if you want to be
pleased

(2)   secrets of which
      he wonders at

(3)   the less guilty elves
      of the Concord Elms
      play around
      his pages

(4)   our music
      is something to do
      with the old hymn tune that haunts the church
      and sings only to those in the churchyard
      to protect them
      from secular noises

      or something to do
      with the concert at the Stamford camp-meeting

      or something to do
      with the Concord he-nymph

      —not something that happens
      but the *way* something happens

or about something that will never happen,

or something else
that is
not

"The Alcotts" . . .

(1)   always *doin'* somethin' —

doin' somethin'
within

(2)   sturdiness and substantial virtues
even if he couldn't
make a living

(3)   under the Concord sky
there sits the little old spinet piano
Sophia Thoreau
gave to the Alcott children
on which Beth
played at the *Fifth Symphony* . . .

a common interest:
in common things and common men —a tune
the Concord bards are ever playing

while they pound away at the immensities
with a Beethoven-like sublimity

(4)   not much
      besides the memory
      of that house
      under the elms . . .

      in this world,
      in the next

Thoreau . . .

(1)   not because he
      played the flute,

      but because he . . .

(2)   miles of space
      intervene
      between men

      measure
      the solitude

(3)   grass from Iceland
      could be found
      in Concord

in which an ode
to morning
is sung

(4) let Nature
put him
under her microscope
than hold her
under his

(5) inside work
out-of-doors

and time from
demands
of *time*

(6) forty thousand souls
at a ball game
rubbing elbows
don't bring men's minds
closer together

neither is there safety
in stupidity
alone

(7) forgive him saying:
     I love my friends, I
     find it of no use to see them

     I hate them
     commonly
     when I am
     near
     the whole outside universe
     of personalities

(8) his *today*:
     a mood of yesterday

     a contradiction
     tomorrow

(9) "the solitary example of
     one sincere life . . ."

     the arc
     for the circle . . .

     yes, he could have been
     more generous
     to society—

     less need of it
     than most

(10) this man's intimacy
       with God —
       as if he had a monopoly
       on the subject

       not that the ship was sinking
       but that *he* was

(11) have virtue
       and men will pursue

       and the people
       with their dirty institutions
       will be
       virtuous,

       does he not say?

(12) economic noise
       takes care of itself;

       dissonances are becoming beautiful! —

       the same waters that roar
       in a storm
       take care of
       the eventual
       calm

(13) someone asked Thoreau
     if he found it lonely there

     only by your help said
     the Visionary Sore-Head

(14) they remind us
     that he died of consumption
     but forget that
     he lived with consumption —

     these people who will die literally,
     and with the pedal loud

(15) follow him
     some spring morning
     to Baker Farm:

     pine groves
     so soft and green and shady
     Druids would
     forsake their oaks
     to worship
     in them

(16) many in Concord
     knew that within their village
     there was a tree
     of wondrous growth,
     the shadow of which,
     alas,
     the only part
     they were allowed
     to touch

(17) you know your Thoreau —
     but not my Thoreau

     one low day
     the sun
     had gone down,
     long, long
     before sunset . . .

     you know him not
     unless you love him!

(18) he knows now
      he must let Nature
      flow through *him*
      and slowly
      in revery
      amidst goldenrod, sandcherry
      and sumac
      he grew
      in those seasons
      like corn in the night
      better than any
      works of the hand

      it was morning
      and lo! now it is evening

      nothing memorable
      accomplished

(19) darker

      the poet's flute
      is heard

      out over
      the pond

Epilogue . . .

(1)   and to the rest of our friends:
      a series of unpleasant sounds

(2)   can he paint
      the setting sun?

(3)   a man remembers his father
      just returned from a performance of *Siegfried*,
      ashamed of enjoying the music
      as he did . . .

      the love was
      make-believe;
      the passion
      :all make-believe,

      as was the dragon

(4)   former beauty and nobility
      were not there

      and in their place
      stood irritating intervals
      of descending fourths and fifths

something in us
has made us flow past him
and not he
past us

(5)   Bach and Beethoven
are also being flowed past—

not as fast perhaps
as Wagner is

as well as
it can be measured

(6)   perhaps the being nearer God or being
nearer the devil?—

process:
unknown

(7)   we do not know that all this is so,
but we feel that it is so

nobody knows
except those serious writers of humorous essays
in art magazines,

who demonstrate for all time and men
that beauty is a quadratic monomial—

that is *is* absolute —
that it *is* relative —
that it is *not* relative —
that it is *not* . . .

(8)   we prefer to go around
      in a circle
      than around
      in a parallelepipedon

      we prefer
      Whittier to
      Baudelaire

      a healthy
      to a
      rotten apple

      we like the beautiful

      we are glad the beautiful
      is not ugly

      having unsettled
      what beauty is
      let us
      go on . . .

(9)   what you are
      talks so loud
      that I cannot hear
      what you say

      first dull,
      then dark,
      then dead

(10) after all is said and sung
      he will find that his music is American
      (assuming he is an American)

      there is good authority
      an African soul under X ray
      looks identically
      like an American soul

(11) he finds in them —
      some of them —
      a vigor, a depth of feeling,
      a natural-soil rhythm,
      a sincerity —
      emphatic but inartistic —
      which, in spite of vociferous sentimentality,
      carries him nearer
      the "Christ of the People"
      than does the *Te Deum*
      of the greatest cathedral

(12) local color, national color, any color
     is a pigment of
     the universal color

(13) if Debussy
     had hoed corn
     or sold newspapers
     for a living

     he might have gained
     a deeper vitality

     to sing at night
     and of a Sunday

     Debussy,
     that city man,
     who comes out for a Sunday
     in the country . . .

(14) perfect media—
     those perfect instruments
     of getting in the way of
     perfect truths

(15) the waiter brings the only fresh egg he has,
     but the man at breakfast
     sends it back
     because it doesn't fit his eggcup!

My God! what has sound
got to do with music!

why can't music
go out
in the same way
it comes in
to a man,
without having to crawl
over a fence of sounds,
thoraxes, catguts, wire, wood, and brass?

is it the composer's fault
that a man
has only ten fingers?

silence
is a solvent . . .

(16) in the same state of mind
you'll be in
when you look down
and see the sexton
keeping your tombstone
up to date

(17) a man may
    become famous because
    he is able
    to eat nineteen
    dinners a day

    posterity will salute his stomach,
    not his brain

(18) the moment
    a famous violinist
    refused to 'appear'
    until he had received his check —
    at that moment — precisely —
    at that moment
    he became but a man
    of 'talent'

(19) music may yet be *unborn* . . .

    the best product that human beings can boast of
    is probably Beethoven;

    maybe his art is nothing
    in comparison with the future product
    of some coal-miner's soul
    in the forty-first
    century . . .

(20) the Country
     has not been waiting for anybody—

     we have many Moses
     always with us

(21) messages that speed
     right through the minds and hearts
     without as much
     splattering the wall

     things
     everybody has
     seen, known and heard
     since Rome
     or Man
     fell

     o politico eloquence!
     always some
     who will buy
     anything

(22) to see the sun rise
     a man has
     but
     to get up
     early

he can always have
Bach
in his pocket

(23) it's possible
a day in a Kansas wheatfield
might do more for
a candidate of Clio's
than three years
in Rome

art's air
might be a little
clearer

(24) ragtime has its uses,
as the cruet on the boarding-house table has—

but to plant a whole farm
with sunflowers,
to put a sunflower
into every bouquet would be
calling Nature
something worse than
a politician

(25) better than bad music
is no music

(26) all occupations
     of man's soul and body
     in their diversity
     come from but one
     soul and body

     a highbrow can always whip
     a lowbrow

     John L. Sullivan
     was a highbrow

(27) better to go to the plate
     and strike out
     than to hold the bench
     down

       than let the ears
       lie back
       in an easy chair

(28) flabbier and flabbier
     over and over
     an overdose of tried-out delight . . .

       result:
       the musical-muscle of his clientele
       gives way altogether

in the
transcendent,
habit-forming,
seasoned
opera box

(29) Beethoven had to pull the ear, *hard*,
and in the same place and several times,
for the 1790 was tougher than
the 1890 one . . .

if Nature is not enthusiastic
about explanation
why should
Tschaikowsky be?

(30) now:
speculations less
speculative

like the sad thoughts
of a bathtub
when the water
is being let out . . .

(31) cherished thoughts, sacred communities
now vanished,

yet America is not too young
to have its divinities
beneath our Concord elms —

of humblest clay
"instinct with celestial fire"

(32) that hog-hearted impulse to be *recognized*
        as a genius —
not to *be* one . . .

ENGLAND AND THE DALES

BLUE BALL BLUES
(for Paul Goodman)

O, Mr. Chemist, please let me buy
350 pounds of premium Kentucky KY,

cause it's a dry season
for the reason

Anglo-Saxon sex glands
are awry . . .

Arise, arise and come
to Perineum

*("the more you come
the more you can")*

Let not your Sword sleep in your Hand
and we shall smear Petroleum
on England's Groin
& Pleasant Gland!

TWO PASTORALS FOR SAMUEL PALMER
AT SHOREHAM, KENT:

1. "IF THE NIGHT COULD GET UP & WALK"

I cannot put my hand into
a cabbage to turn
on the light, but

the moon moves over
the field of dark cabbage and an
exchange fills
all veins.

The cabbage is also a globe
of light, the two globes

now two eyes in
my saturated

head!

2. "ONE MUST TRY BEHIND THE HILLS"

Eight Great Dahlias stood
beyond the Mountains

they set fire to the Sun
in a black wood
beyond the Mountains,

in the Valley of Vision

the Fission of
Flowers

yields all Power
in the Valley of Vision

eight Suns,
on eight Stems,

aflame!

____

Readers are referred to Geoffrey Grigson's two books: Samuel Palmer's Valley of Vision *(Phoenix House, 1960)* and Samuel Palmer: The Visionary Years *(Routledge, 1947). My titles are from letters by Palmer to George Richmond.*

THE FOURTEEN-YEAR-OLD
SAMUEL PALMER'S WATERCOLOUR
NOTATIONS FOR THE SKETCH,
"A LANE AT THANET":

> grey sky
> mottled with blue &
> warmish light

this thatch
very bright

> > elder
> > berry very bright

> this
> little
> gate

> very bright

> > br. light

Palmer's sketchbook of 1819 has recently been acquired by the British Museum from the great-grandson of his younger brother, William. It has glimmerings of the visionary Blakean style evidenced in the famous sketchbook of 1824, and of the paintings in the "Valley of Vision," on the Darenth, Kent, 1824–34.

REFLECTIONS FROM "APPALACHIA"
(In Honor of Delius's Centenary: 1962)

dawn songs in the dews of young orange trees;
and ranging orisons; and wordless longings

sung in tranquillity's waters sliding in sun's
light;

and benisons sung in these trees . . .

in these, yes, it is the "ah-ness," yes, it is the
     course of adrenalin,
but, it is the lens opening of Frederick Delius'
     luminous blind eye:
f/stop open—
all things measureless lucidities,

my eyes
so in tune: atonement, at-one-ment is
atonement,

what is meant by not
being able to focus two eyes . . .

they lie on the horizon,
they lie on the great St. John's River's waters
in the monocular sunlight

three miles wide
lid to lid

THE WRECK ON THE A-222 IN RAVENSBOURNE VALLEY

*"There are more things to love than we could
dare to hope for."*
                    —Richard of Saint Victor

where the car hit him, fireweed sprang with
blazons of fennel

and umbels
of dill fell
through the spokes of a wheel

on Whitsun holiday to the sun, Denton
Welch spun a web in his crushed cycle,

sat in the seat, spine curled up like a spider—

and spied: "saw
            the very drops of sweat glittering frostily
            between the shoulder blades"

            of a lad

. . . on and on he spied and bled from the blades
      of his cycle,
small as a spider,
hiding in the fireweed, getting
wet from the skins of many human suns aground
at the Kentish river near
Tunbridge Wells,

where the dill
lulls,

and all boys
spoil . . .

---

*The dire chronicle of Denton Welch's (1917–1948) accident and illness
is told in* A Voice Through a Cloud, *originally published by John
Lehmann in Great Britain and recently republished in America by the
University of Texas Press.*

DIRGE FOR SEER-SCRIVENER, PRINCE-PLANGENT OF GORMENGHAST

"And the days move on
and the names of the months change
and the four seasons bury one another
and the field-mice draw upon their granaries"

—this is the kind of vision
Mervyn Peake shares with William Blake:

seeing
not with
but *thru*
the eye!

you get it, very very steady
in the *Titus* trilogy—

one extraordinary instance being
that passage in Book One—pp. 116.7,
where Steerpike spies the dead tree
high on the cyclopean walls
of Gormenghast Castle;

and in Book Two, Chapter Fifty-One, Section V:

"... *A loosened stone falls from a high tower.*
A fly drops lifeless from a broken pane.
A sparrow twitters in a cave of ivy ..."

I can do nothing but quote
this fantastic man, like Kenneth Patchen,
creator of one Dark Kingdom,
unstrung by a darker one ...

I lament all ravens and the owls in hell
who stay his hand
and dis-connect this sun

Mervyn Peake (1911-died November 17, 1968, at Burcot, Oxfordshire) was perhaps the last master of gothic delineation and the grotesque, though his prose comes from Melville and Dickens and not Mrs. Radcliffe. Because of his disabling psychic illnesses we had no successors to the Gormenghast Trilogy *or to such illustrations as those to the "Ancient Mariner" or to* Alice in Wonderland. *Like Delius, Poe, Lovecraft, Coleridge, his time was no place for him.*

THE TRIUMPH OF CRAFT: A VIGNETTE
FROM THE HEBRIDES FOR A HOME ARTS &
INDUSTRIES EXHIBITION AS ARRANGED BY
MARY FRAZER-TYTLER WATTS UNDER THE
ELMS AT COMPTON, SURREY:

lad asks Bessie
the old lady
in the factory

well then, what do you do
with all that steel wool
you steal?

well then,
I'm knittin'
a kettle

Mary Watts, the young second wife of G.F. Watts, painter and Honorary President of the Anti-Tight-Lacing Society (Gertie Tipple, Secretary), in her designs for the Watts Memorial Chapel at Compton, near Guilford, Surrey, created one of the unique fantasies in all of architecture: Celtic plus Art Nouveau plus Obsessive Theosophical . . . Watts, himself, needs revision on the basis of such paintings as "The Sower of Systems," where he comes out minor-league Gustave Moreau. And, after all, to quote the authoritative words of Violet A. Wlock, B.A., Deputy Curator of the Castle Museum, York, 1939–47, in her "A Chat on the Valentine": ". . . crinolines are creeping their way to fashion, there is even a whisper of tight lacing . . ."

A YELL FOR THE GREATEST
TERRIBLE WRITER IN THE WORLD:

AMANDA! AMANDA!
SIS-BOOM-BAH!

McKITTRICK! McKITTRICK!
RAH-RAH-RAH!

ROS! ROS!
THE REST IS DROSS!

Jack Loudan's biography, O Rare Amanda! *(Chatto, 1954), is the proper introduction to the magisterial alliterations of Amanda McKittrick Ros (1860–1939). There is nothing else like this tea-cozy prose from Larne Harbor, County Antrim, Ulster. Read* Irene Iddesleigh, Delina Delaney, *and* Poems of Puncture. *Here is a quite ordinary passage from* Helen Huddleston: *"Helen Huddleston's cleanly vessels were never smeared with the abominable phlegm of the profligate . . . her tiny feet always pattered on the pavements of the pure." My discovery of Amanda I owe to Arthur Uphill, of London, a rare and honored friend.*

MISERICORD (1)

a dignified figure
seated at a desk
with a large bird
beside her
and the head
of either a snake
or a small dog
emerging from the sleeve
of her loose robe

MISERICORD (2)

virago
in a barrow

MISERICORD (3)

hammering a wedge
to split
a hedge-stake

MISERICORD (4)

his right hand
is broadcasting seed

a horse
walks behind

MISERICORD (5)

what
no doubt
was a hawk

on his wrist

MISERICORD (6)

two men
hold partly filled sacks
and a long corn bin
as they kneel behind
a pile of grain

"AND HE HATH SOWN . . ."

and he hath sown pese benes
and such things as those

he hath made the dounghill
something less than it was

A DALESMAN CONSIDERS
EDGAR ALLAN POE'S ASSERTION THAT
CELLARDOOR IS THE MOST BEAUTIFUL
WORD IN THE LANGUAGE AND COMES UP
WITH THE MEDIAEVAL NAME OF THE
VALLEY OF THE WHIRLING, SPLASHING
RIVER BETWEEN REETH AND RICHMOND:

SUALADALA

GEORGE FOX

(moved to open to the people
that the steeple-house
and the ground where-on —
no more holy
than a mountain)

speaks from a stone on
Firbank Fell by

Crockaloyne

A GLIMPSE OF THE SECRET PATH
FROM HILL TOP FARM TO THE DOOR IN THE
BACK OF THAT HILL CALLED CATBELLS,
USED BY BEATRIX POTTER TO VISIT
DEAR MRS. TIGGY-WINKLE

A SERIES OF FIVE CHARRED, BLACKENED LUMPS SERVED AS "MIXED GRILL" BY THE HIGH FORCE HOTEL, UPPER TEASDALE, COUNTY DURHAM

From the Shapes, Please Tell Us Which Are:

(1)   the Sausage

(2)   the Lamb Chop

(3)   the Mushroom

(4)   The Tomato

(5)   The Kidney

FULL-FRONTAL CARD OF MR. E. M. FORSTER BEING TOUCHED ON THE BUTTOCKS BY EDWARD CARPENTER'S URANIAN FRIEND, GEORGE MERRILL, IN THE GREENWOOD NEAR MILNTHORPE, DERBYSHIRE, IN 1913

Line Drawing Indicates Path of the Sensation
From the Back
(Figure A)

Into the Ideas
(Figure B).

BROWSING THROUGH *PLAYBOY*
MAGAZINE'S ADVICE COLUMN IN A
SUMMER GARDEN ALONG OUGHTERSHAW
BECK, ONE ENCOUNTERS A PRIME
INSTANCE OF WHAT THE GERMANS CALL
DIE WISSENSCHAFT DES NICHT WISSEN-
WERTEN, "THE SCIENCE OF WHAT IS NOT
WORTH KNOWING":

    there being only 2 calories
    in the average ejaculation
    of semen

    oragenitalists should
    limit their daily consumption
    to less than
    700 times a day

    in order to comply
    with the demands
    of the BBC's dietary programme
    "NATIONWIDE SLIM 72"

RICHARD BRATHWAITE, OF
WESTMORLAND, REPORTS
IN A TREATISE ON CIVILITY FROM 1630
THAT THE TONGUE
IS A SMALL MEMBER, BUT
VERY GLIBBERY

THREE LIMERICKS FOR THE THREE PEAKS

assessing the angle of Ingleborough
caused Cotman to dangle his single bore
in a glish bit of clay,
mixed with Paine's grey,
he kept in a monochrome shingle burrow

Edward Lear was the sort of gent
whose spelling was reet-frabjous-bent:
"the venue for fine weekend sin
is either a far mouse or a ninn,"
he chortled—and sidled up Penyghent

Turner was fast to decide
mountains were groovy when spied . . .
"to feel real sublime
is worth the glum climb
to get to the tarns up on Whernside"

A NOTICE IN EIRE

Ladies & Gentlemen will not
and others must not
pull the Flowers in this Garden

THE INTAKE AT OUGHTERSHAW

the
    little
        field

that
    Matt
        had

LES VACANCES DE JOCK TATTIE

LOCH, N'EST-CE PAS?

THE REVEREND SEPTIMUS BUSS
MEETS THE GREAT NORWEGIAN LINGUIST
SOPHUS BUGGE
ON THE CRAGS OF CRAIG YR YSFA
AND MUTTERS ABOUT THE PREVIOUS
DAY'S FISHING
IN THE AFON LLUGWY
BELOW THE SWALLOW FALLS:

cowt
nowt
nobbut
newts

OUTDOOR GAMES NEAR WASHINGTON NEW TOWN

one young lady
about eight
solemnly asks the venerable poet:
Mr. Bunting,
are you God?

next time out
the grandfatherly poet
puts in his contact
lenses manufactured by the C. L. Dodgson Co. Ltd
and strolls up the road
in Black Fell

when he strokes and tosses
the golden curls of an angelic lass
of about three years
who looks straight from a passage
by Sir Joshua Reynolds,
or even from Fra Angelico,
she turns around, hoists her knickers
and says:
fook off,
you silly booger!

MY QUAKER-ATHEIST FRIEND,
WHO HAS COME TO THIS MEETING-HOUSE
    SINCE 1913,
SMOKES
& LOOKS OUT OVER THE RAWTHEY
    TO HOLME FELL:

what do you do
anything for?

you do it
for what the mediaevals would call
something like
the *Glory of God*

doing it for money,
that doesn't do it;

doing it for vanity,
that doesn't do it;

doing it to justify a disorderly life,
that doesn't do it

Look at Briggflatts here . . .

It represents the best
that the people were able to do

they didn't do it for gain;
in fact, they must have
taken a loss

whether it is a stone next to a stone
or a word next to a word,
it is the *glory*—
the simple craft of it

and money and sex aren't worth
bugger-all, not
bugger-all

solid, common, *vulgar* words

the ones you can touch,
the ones that yield

and a respect for the music . . .

what else can you tell 'em?

THE SEXUAL STRUT

THE LOOK-OUT TOWER
AT MOUNT VENUS, LOUISIANA

yes yes o lord yes, the bestest, sweetest
pussy
        ever said good-morning to a slop-jar!

you know:
            "nappy" pussy,
like counting
prayer-beads:

. . . . ( ) . . . .

Heard/found-object, from Clement, manservant to Weeks Hall, at the latter's plantation, The Shadows-on-the-Teche, New Iberia, Louisiana, 1957.

THE CHAMELEON

at 14 I decided it was avant-garde to dig
women

but, man if I were just the least
bit queer, boy, you know, man, wow,

and then some; but, like
I'm not, but

when I write *Dearest* to you in a letter, then
that's different,

isn't it?

A LITTLE TUMESCENCE

this time, I mean it:
twice tonight!

        (*omne animal*, always
        The Hope

triste, triste
situation, such outrageous
limitation,
limp,

    simply

The rooster, post-coitum, is an exception—it laughs.

OVID, MEET A METAMORPHODITE

Hermaphroditus, a delight, a
dreamboat on Lake Salmacis,

a dazzling dud
what wist not whut luv wuz

alas, a lout, the lass aloud allowed,
                              so far beside herself

that scarcely could she stay

so Sister Salmacis hides her in
a bushy queach
to glim the scene at Muscle-Beach
as Hermes, Junior, doffs
his dongarees

no fenny sedge, nor barren reek, no reed
nor rush, just

SPLASH!

—and passion's double-clutched!

strive, writhe, wrest and struggle,
        unsnugglin' stranger, grins she
snake-like,
applyin' the boa bit . . .

Hermaphroditus?/Hismaphroditus?
butch?/bitch?
which twain has the gonē?

o, one'll get you two: a toy of double-shape—

the cream of
genes!

THE HONEY LAMB

the boysick (by gadzooks thunderstruck)
Rex Zeus, sex
expert, erects
a couple temples
                  and cruises the Trojan Coast . . .

eagle-eyed, spies,
swoops,
swishes into town

ponders, whether tis nobler
to bullshit, brown
or go down
on
    that catamite cat, Kid Ganymedes,
                              mead-mover,

erstwhile eagle-scout
bed-mate

HISTORY VII:

                                        to sleep naked

with a naked friend

MARCH 5:

clean sheets,
just in case

"FOUR-WAY GAY"
(VERSION FOR ENGLISH COUNTRY GENTS)

Dave and Jack;
Rick and Jim;

Dave and Rick;
Jim and Jack;

Jim and Dave;
Jack and Rick —

plus fours!

HOMAGE TO R. CRUMB,
THE "CRUMMY GOYA,"
THE "RUNNY GOYIM"

hot springs
it says
on newly weds' bumpers

spring came running
down your thigh

from how high?

from honey on
the moon,
honey . . .

such tunes,
such tunes,

such tunes will make
your boogie

ooze

SYMPHONIC DANCES, OPUS 45

Lento assai:

a sigh
in the wind

being
the wind
and what it did
to the underside
of the pine needles

and the Ruysdael clouds
and the blond hair of the boy from Penland

that,
on top of
Italian salami, Tom's French bread,
devilled eggs, cold Buds,
and the swim
in the waterfall—

this is called,
O Best Beloveds,
getting it all
together

leave a place for our friends
wild ginger
and galax,
and the lassitude
of bees

and this is as
together
as it
gets

"ACTUALLY, I DIDN'T COME OUT
OF THE CLOSET UNTIL 1971"

        8-foot
buck-toothed
        southern

gurl

DOMESTIC BLISS AMONGST THE CELTIC
BRIGANTES OF WEST RIDING
(In the Holy Catfish Manner of Joe Brainard)

behind the marquetry panel
of the oak court-cupboard in the bedroom in
        Dentdale
(the panel with the diamond
of ebony, holly, and mahogany,
dated 1636)

we keep our collection
of pillow books

my current rousing literary favorites are:
Naked on Main Street, by Richard Amory; and
Hang-Up, by James Colton

sympathetic, refined WASP types—one's going into
    forestry,
one plays concert piano

no *Spiders from Mars*, no Iggy Pop,
no Alice Cooper, no yobbos from
Mr. Burroughs's heavy-metal vomitorium

Mr. Amory is a practised hand,
with a deft touch.
I was glad to learn
he wasn't W.H. Auden.

the best one is
The Homosexual Marriage.
I bought it all sealed up
from a Catholic, Spanish-American lady
in the bus station in Santa Fe
for $5.95.
Good value. Definitely worth it.
The text is also edifying,
if you want advice about
whether to have a gay tree-surgeon or not,
and it's written by a Ph.D.,
to keep up the low moral tone.

it's those two boys
at the beginning—
whether it's just all the California orange juice,
    who can say,
but they are really into each other

usual motel decor,
except there is this
curious wallpaper
like a James McGarrell painting
in some of the shots—

like Captain Beefheart's privates,
row on row,
or maybe they're niggerhearts,
like in Zap Comix?—

"Oh, Mommy,
let's have Niggerhearts for dinner!"

anyway, they're into everything
randy
and the scene with the brunet
sitting on the blond's chest
pumping it in deeply
past those lips
hanging back over the edge of the bed

while his buddy
brings a hand-job to the boil —
that's very affecting . . .

one enters the picture,
gets between his legs
in no time
flat

I also like the worn jeans
on the floor, the way
they're frayed

the darker boy
wouldn't wear
shorts

very cocky, very spunky
he is

nice to see kids whose eyes glitter
for each other,
not (necessarily) for the 50 bucks
they might have got
from some saurian photographer

the other scopophiliac toilers in the book are
        tacky Europeans

with tattoos, crew-cuts, kinky undershirts, cheap
metal-banded watches, vulgar rings, and even socks
they never take off—
they're just so much salami

my boys,
call them Tim and Mike
(they're nothing classy like Garvin and Anthony),
never tire of it
on their long long weekends away from UCLA
where they're Pre-Law undergraduates
with their eye on a job
with the old established firm of
Fuck Suck Rim & Blow

it's nice to make it with them
now and then,

when Tom's downstairs
reading Wittgenstein

Ach, Mein Herz, out in the wide world
there are these ephebes

who keep away the general freeze,
who make your knees crack
when you come

but, mostly, we stay home
and let our imaginations roam

Tom
likes them
too

BENEDICTINE
(for JHW)

Father Odo
of Cluny

(Third Abbot)

was wont to say

womankind is a
sacca stercoris

womankind is a
bag of shit

meaning, shucks, he could not bring himself to voice
the sibilant Mediaeval word for *merde*
and had to retreat into a distant, foreign,
        and sonorous tongue

even today
in these eschatological times
some people couldn't say SHIT
if they had a mouth full

AMORI ET DOLORI SACRUM
(for Comte Jacques d'Adelsward-Ferson)

    boys
    will be
    boys'

PLAIN, ABSOLUTELY UNREFINED

    yessir buddy
    three moon pies and a nehi
    grape

you see them five boys
on that fence across the street
hangin out actin cute

reckon i could fuck
every last mothers son in
just one week

if i was lucky
and had me maybe just one more
moon pie

HEADMASTER

in the school greenhouse,
chicken loft, stables, cellar and
swimming pool filter house

in the study, in the car,
in bedrooms and in bathrooms

ROB

at home
in his room

PAINTING THE DAISIES WITH LARRY

I'd love to be
his jockey shorts
on Friday night

VICTORIA WOOD, IN "TALENT":

I always thought
coq au vin

was
love in a lorry

RAINY DAY AT MISS FIST'S

coloring in
the coloring book . . . .

LES CHAMPS ELYSÉES
DE LA GRANDE CUISINE
(Homage to Fernand Point)

farmboysin

framboises

KEVIN

he says
he's straight

A BRIGHTON BELLE

she's black with ten
inches

I'm green with en-
vy

ON THE FUEL TANK, RED BULL WHARF

smile,
if you had it last night

laugh,
if you didn't

A WEE TOT FOR CATULLUS

eye laddie!

JOCK STRAP
TRAPS JOCK

(((((((((catso
fatso)))))))))

IN MARSDEN HARTLEY'S HAND

happily contented
to be climbing the heights and the clouds
by the brush method

•

they
have to
come of
themselves

•

place me in the middle
between these lovers of mine
and there you have us

•

goldenglories
of my heart's gate

•

I see
the mail carrier
coming down
the field

●

I know
what I see

●

to walk on
throughout the exquisite days
with you

enough that you
call me brother,
friend, lover

a kiss
to you
across
these
isolated hills

●

one can't have all
things in the hills

yet I found your letter
here in the hills

.

better
to be walking about
with new young stars
in one's hand
than fumbling over
old meteors

.

a big broad shoulder
to brush by . . . .

the flicker
of the yellow butterfly . . . .

.

somehow
this business of one
isn't big enough

•

love again,
always love

THE LAST WANK
OF MAJOR WEDGWOOD-WANKER

old
china
hand

job

A T-SHIRT FOR THE SHOCK TROOPS OF
GENERAL WILDE IN THE FORTHCOMING
WAR AGAINST THE MULIERISTS:

S O M D O M I T E   M I G H T

JARGON SOCIETY POSTCARD NO. 16
HIGHLANDS, NORTH CAROLINA 28741
BARON CORVO'S BIRTHDAY,

AMANITA/ANITA INDUSTRIES
present

C L O N E   C O L O G N E

"Smell Just Like Everybody Else
On The Seventh Circle Of Hell,"
As You Walk With Your Baby,
Down By The San Francisco Bay. . . .

WORKSOP, NOTTS.

your brothers never used to do it
just look at those sheets
I ought to rub your nose in it

A DEMOCRACY OF CONTENT; OR, "SOME PEOPLE WOULD WRITE ABOUT ANYTHING"

O FOR A MUSE OF FIRE!

Date: Tuesday, May 13, 1958 —
    a date previously memorable in history for the
        birth of
    Joe Louis (1914),
    the Empress Maria Theresa (1717),
    and the beheading of
    Johan Van Olden Barnveldt (1619)

Place: Wrigley Field, Chicago, Illinois

Time: 3:06 p.m.; warm and sunny; breeze steady,
        right to left

Attendance: 5,692 (paid)

Situation: top of the sixth; Cardinals trailing the Cubs,
        3–1: one out; Gene Green on 2nd

Public Address: "Batting for Jones, #6, Stan Musial!"

The Muse muscles up; Stan the Man stands in . . . and
O, Hosanna, Hosanna, Ozanna's boy, Moe Drabowsky
    comes in

2 and 2
"a curve ball, outside corner, higher
than intended—
I figured he'd hit it in the ground"

("it felt fine!")

a line shot to left, down the line,
rolling deep for a double . . .

("it felt fine!")

Say, Stan, baby, how's it feel to hit 3000?

"Uh, it feels fine"

Only six major-league players in baseball history had hit safely 3000 times prior to this occasion. The density of the information surrounding the event continues to surprise me, rather belies Tocqueville's assertion that Americans cannot concentrate.

THE ADHESIVE AUTOPSY
OF WALT WHITMAN

"Gentlemen, look on this wonder . . .
and wonders within there yet":

"pleurisy of the left side, consumption
of the right lung,

general miliary tuberculosis
and parenchymatous nephritis . . . a fatty

liver, a huge stone
filling the gall,

a cyst in the adrenal, tubercular abscesses
involving the bones,

and pachymeningitis"

"that he was a Kosmos is a piece of news we were
hardly prepared for . . ."

Verbatim quotations from the Philadelphia and Camden newspapers.

A VULNERARY
(for Robert Duncan)

one comes to language from afar, the ear
fears for its sound-barriers —

but one "comes"; the language "comes" for
The Beckoning Fair One

*plant you now, dig you
later*, the plaint stirs winter
earth . . .

air in a hornets' nest
over the water makes a
solid, six-sided music . . .

a few utterly quiet scenes, things
are very far away — *"form
is emptiness"*

comely, comely, love trembles

and the sweet-shrub

THE ANCHORITE

quotes Basil Bunting from "Chomei at Toyama":
if you can keep straight you will have no friends
but catgut and blossom in season . . .

the anchorite
opts to eye the
oak leaf, clutch
a red
to hold the mountains' blues
under the winter sun . . .

song accumulates heat—a humus. I have it,
like Issa:

> *Few people;*
> *a leaf falls here,*
> *falls there*

> —outside, where
> the world's a storm
> in the oaks

> and the outcry of certain
> beautiful captures

•

he wrote 'brought to love,' brought to any
intimacy,
          writing letters
among red oak leaves . . .

to be left alone? — that's a laugh! that is, who's
without the images of
love,
      shining out of his head?

and they
who move the heart, daringly,
as the sun fires the oak
through the wanton afternoon
•

light airs of music . . .

we are left with
just the "facts," the endless

articulation

SYMPHONY NO. 5, IN C SHARP MINOR

"How blessed, how blessed a tailor to be!
Oh that I had been born a commercial traveller
and engaged as baritone at the Opera! Oh that
I might give my Symphony its first performance
fifty years after my death!"—Mahler, 1904

I. FUNERAL MARCH

Mahler, from his studio on the 11th floor of the
Hotel Majestic, New York City, hears the cortège of a
fireman moving up Central Park West:

one roll of the drum

one road where the wind storms, where
Cherubim sing birds' songs
with human faces and hold the world
in human hands and
drift on the gold road
where black wheels smash
all

one roll of the drum

II. STORMILY AGITATED

to be a block of flowers
in a wood

to be mindlessly in flower
past understanding

to be shone on
endlessly

to be *there*, there
and blessed

III. SCHERZO

one two three
one two three

little birds waltz to and fro
in the piano

at Maiernigg on the
Wörthersee

and up the tree:
cacophony

one two three

IV. ADAGIETTO

one feels
one clematis petal
fell

its circle
is all

glimmer on this pale
river

V. RONDO-FINALE

Schoenberg: "I should
even have liked to observe
how Mahler
knotted his tie,

and should have found that
more interesting and instructive
than learning how
one of our musical bigwigs composes
on a quote sacred subject
unquote

. . . An apostle
who does not glow
preaches heresy."

his tie was knotted
with éclat
on the dead run!

FOUND POEM NUMBER 1

(FIFTH GENERAL HOSPITAL, BAD CANNSTATT/
STUTTGART, 1953: THE SPEAKER, A BOP SPADE
FROM CLEVELAND IN A FUGUE STATE, MAKING
THE WORLD'S FIRST MARRIAGE OF THE POETICS
OF CHARLES OLSON AND DAME EDITH SITWELL—
AND YOU ARE THERE!)

man,
i come from
the 544
            motherfuckin'
                        double-clutchin'
                                    cocksuckin'
truckin' company!

U CALL—
WE HAUL
U ALL . . .

we got
2 plys
    4 plys
        6 plys
            8 plys, semi's—

and them BIG motherfuckers
go

CHEW!
CHEW!

ORANGE COUNTY BLUES
(To the Tune: "Keep Your Chicken Lickin' ")

fresh, ford-run-over
possum
plus a six-pak

that's the springtime seven-coarse greasy spoon
        blue-plate
special in Chapel
Hill according to Bill
Harmon, poet & possum
consumer

this spring weather's
tough on possums

they get out in the middle lane
and just get nicked
and take a long time to succumb

the possum,
like the literary life,
it's a little rank
lately . . .

SWEET AIRES THAT GIVE DELIGHT
(for Joseph Pujol, Le Petomane)

there was an Old Fart from Toulon
whose pet sphincter was known as "Ptomaine" . . .
sur la terrasse
it could really tear-ass
and enchantingly blast *Clair de Lune*

FROM THE TALMUD

Britisher
was in the cab
the other day

said
I hear New York's
getting better

I said
you kidding

this
isn't
New York

this
used to be
New York

FRUITS CONFITS

neck tureen

•

turtle nectarine

•

liszt tureen

•

noct-urine
(alias, Chopin's Chamber Pot)

•

baba
  au
rhum
  ba

•

les poèmes de terre au dactyles

•

soccer torte

•

H. Ombre
(a.k.a. "The Shadow," man)

•

pool ankh

•

Ma Gritte and
Pa Gritte greet
Maupassant
en passant

dans Passy
au tombeau
de De-
bussy

THE ANTHROPOPHAGITES GET DOWN
ON A BARBECUE SIGN ON
HIGHWAY NC 107 SOUTH OF HAMLET

EAT
300 FEET

SHOTGUN SHUBA THINKS
MIDDLE-AGED SLOVAKIAN THOUGHTS
ABOUT THE DODGERS
ONE EVENING IN OHIO
ALONG THE MAHONING RIVER:

what
does it mean?
it doesn't mean
much

Ruth died.
Gehrig died.

a long way,
a long time ago . . .

Typeset at NewComp Graphics Center, a part of
Beyond Baroque Foundation, partially funded by
the National Endowment for the Arts.